Debbie Peck

Soft Skills 101
Make Your Message Land

So what you say is
what they understand.

This book isn't about what's broken.

It's about what's possible when we slow down, tune in and communicate with more intention.

The Quiet Cost

I once worked on a project where the person in charge
had the title — but not the skillset.

He'd been promoted into a role he wasn't ready for.
And it showed.

Guarded. Reactive.
More focused on appearances than outcomes.

Maybe it was insecurity or fear of failing.
Maybe he was intent on control, too focused on image
or simply unaware of the effect he was having.

Whatever the cause, the outcome was the same: the team never
really connected.

From day one, I offered to help. To clarify roles.
To connect the dots and move things forward.

But there was no real communication.
No clarity. No collaboration.

Still, I showed up. Did my job. Stayed focused.

But instead of building trust, he built walls —
keeping people at a distance rather than bringing them together.

At meetings, he'd skip over me.
When he did ask for input, he'd scroll his phone while I answered.
No eye contact. No response. Silence.

Eventually, I needed his support — not for me, but for the work.

But in an environment without connection, support wasn't possible — and the project stalled.

Deadlines slipped. Work had to be repeated.

The team wasn't broken — the communication was.

And the cost was real:
Lost time, lost trust and a budget quietly bleeding.

Maybe you've seen it too —
a leader who doesn't realize the gap they're creating.

That experience stayed with me — not as a grudge, but as a wake-up call.

Because this is what happens when soft skills are missing.

Not always dramatic failures.

But the quiet kind — the kind that stall progress, drain morale and cost more than most people realize.

Connection breaks.
Progress slows.

People and companies pay the price.

"The single biggest problem with communication is the *illusion* that it has taken place."

George Bernard Shaw

Why This Book Matters

Miscommunication has a cost.

It rarely shouts. More often it slips in quietly.

An unclear email. A handoff with almost enough detail.
A meeting where clarity gets lost. A question left unasked.

Alone, these misses can seem small. Together, they stall progress.
Time slips. Rework loops. Trust and connection thin.
That is the quiet cost. Time. Rework. Trust. Money.

The answer is not another tool.
It's awareness.

Awareness of what is happening in the exchange — and whether it landed as intended.

That is what soft skills are about — the people skills behind the work.

They are the catalysts that turn awareness into action in the moment:
- Presence to pause before you hit send.
- Empathy to see another's view.
- Emotional awareness to check tone.

Think flywheel:

Clarity fuels trust.
Trust fuels collaboration.
Collaboration fuels results.
Each turn makes the next one easier.

What improves

For you: clearer messages, steadier tone, less friction.
For teams: fewer do-overs, faster decisions, cleaner handoffs.

The Big Bold Promise

When these skills are in play, people communicate with greater clarity, work with less friction and deliver stronger results.

When people and performance thrive, the outcome is stronger teams, better results and a healthier bottom line.

Whether these skills are new to you or already second nature, strengthening them — and noticing them in others — makes work move with more clarity and connection.

You'll spend less time in mix-ups and more time on meaningful work.

Practiced with intention and awareness, these skills reduce guesswork, increase follow-through and improve decisions.

Companies do not run on processes alone.
They run on people.

People thrive when there is trust, respect and the kind of communication that makes them feel valued, motivated to do their best and fulfilled at the end of the day.

What follows are the skills that make communication clearer, relationships stronger and work more rewarding.

Contents

Part Three
Emotional Intelligence and How It Supports Soft Skills

Part Four
The Integration   87

How to use this book...

This is a practical guide—not an exhaustive study.

It focuses on core skills that shape how we work, lead and connect:

- Effective Communication
- Teamwork & Collaboration
- Leadership & Influence
- Adaptability & Flexibility
- Time Management & Organization

Each chapter touches on the everyday behaviors that bring these skills to life—listening, giving feedback, navigating tension, showing up with presence.

You'll also find a short section on emotional intelligence—the self-awareness and steady responses that make these skills actually land.

The pages are short, direct and built for reflection.

Use them as a reference.
A reminder.
A reset.

Flip through or read them in order.
This isn't about doing everything perfectly.

It's about becoming more aware—of yourself, your impact and the way your message lands.

Because when soft skills are in play, people trust you faster, work with you more easily and follow your lead with less resistance.

The outcome is stronger teams, smoother collaboration and a workplace where both performance and people thrive.

PART ONE

Foundations
of
Soft Skills and
Emotional Intelligence

Chapter One

What Soft Skills Are
and
Why They Matter

What Soft Skills Are and Why They Matter

Ever walked away from a conversation thinking, "Wait — that's not what I meant"?

You thought you were clear — but the message didn't land. Now there's confusion, tension or silence.

That's where soft skills come in.
Think of them as people skills — how you connect, communicate and work with others.

They help you get your point across, keep trust intact and solve problems without creating new ones.
They turn good intent into real impact — so nothing gets lost in translation.

What They Are
Soft skills are how you work with people — especially under pressure. They show up in how you listen, give feedback, manage conflict and lead conversations that matter.

They shape how others experience you — and how well you move things forward. They're not about being "nice." They're about being effective — in real moments, with real people.

When they're missing, you feel it. When they're strong, everything else works better.

Why They Matter
Hard skills help you do the job.
Soft skills help you do it with others.

Both are important, but soft skills are what enable hard skills to make an impact — ensuring your work is recognized, valued and acted on.

Here's what that looks like:
- A great idea gains traction because it's communicated clearly
- A tense moment is defused because someone listens first
- A project moves forward because roles are clarified early
- A team stays motivated because trust stays intact

Soft skills reduce friction, strengthen relationships and create the foundation for better communication, stronger teamwork and stronger results — across roles, levels and departments.

The Real Difference
Anyone can learn a task.
The edge comes from how someone shows up, how they lead and how others experience working with them.

That's what sharpening soft skills improves — fast.

They aren't just supportive.
They turn talk into collaboration — and ordinary teams into exceptional ones.

What It Looks Like in Practice
- Listening without interrupting
- Giving clear feedback without shutting people down
- Moving through conflict with steadiness and respect
- Adjusting your tone instead of reacting

<h1 style="text-align:center">If you're curious....</h1>

Where the Term Soft Skills Comes From

The phrase **soft skills** is widely believed to have originated with the U.S. military in the early 1970s.

Leaders noticed that technical training alone wasn't enough — the soldiers who excelled under pressure also had strong people skills. They could communicate, adapt, lead and stay composed in high-stress situations.

At the time, these abilities didn't have a formal name — they were simply seen as essential.

Since **hard skills** already referred to tasks you could train and test — like weapons handling or equipment maintenance — everything else that made someone effective was labeled **soft**.

The skills themselves aren't new — people have always relied on them to work together, solve problems and lead under pressure.

What changed was the label. The military gave these abilities a name in the 1970s and that name stuck.

Today, soft skills are recognized across industries as essential — the human advantage that turns good intent into consistent execution.

Technical skills may get you the job. Soft skills determine how far you'll go.

Unknown

Reflection

- *Think about the term "soft skills" as shorthand for people skills. Everything you read from here forward is about strengthening those skills so we can connect and communicate more effectively.*

- *The reflection pages are simply for awareness. We all drift into autopilot and that's when real moments of connection can slip by. These prompts are just an invitation to pause, notice and see what stands out.*

Soft Skills in Action

A customer's tone is sharp. You don't react. You stay present and tuned in to what's really going on. Your calm makes you approachable and safe, which opens the door to a better conversation and a real fix.

Chapter Two

Emotional Intelligence

Emotional Intelligence

Emotional intelligence (EI) isn't just a theory — it's a real-world skill that shapes how we lead, communicate and connect.

It influences the choices we make, the tone we set and how we respond — especially under pressure.

Emotional intelligence works by increasing your awareness — of yourself, of others and of what's happening in the moment.

That awareness gives you options: to pause, to listen, to shift your approach when needed.

With that clarity, it becomes easier to stay grounded, adapt with intention and respond effectively — even in high-stakes situations.

While this booklet touches on a range of core soft skills, emotional intelligence is what holds them together in practice. It supports clearer communication, deeper trust and more thoughtful collaboration — the kind that drives real progress.

People who intentionally develop their emotional intelligence often experience:
- Stronger relationships
- More effective leadership
- Better decision-making
- Greater trust and respect
- A more consistent presence — especially under pressure

Emotional intelligence isn't fixed. It's a skill you strengthen — with awareness, reflection and consistent practice.

The more intentional you are, the more naturally it shows up — and the safer others feel to speak up, contribute and connect.

And it's often in the smallest moments — the pause before reacting, the effort to truly listen — that emotional intelligence makes the biggest difference.

The Four Components of Emotional Intelligence

These four core components, popularized by Psychologist Daniel Goleman, offer a clear framework for recognizing emotions, responding with empathy and navigating relationships with greater confidence and care.

As you move through the soft skills ahead, you'll start to see how each one connects back to these core abilities — and how building EI strengthens everything from how you listen to how you lead.

Each one builds on the others — and together, they form the foundation of strong leadership and communication.

Self-awareness

The ability to recognize and understand your own emotions, thought patterns and personal triggers. *This includes being honest with yourself and recognizing how your feelings influence your behavior and decisions.*

Self-management

The skill of managing emotions — especially in moments of stress or uncertainty. *It involves staying grounded, thinking clearly and choosing a thoughtful response over a reactive one.*

Social awareness

The ability to sense the emotions of others and understand the tone and energy of a group. *This includes reading nonverbal cues, listening actively and recognizing the dynamics as they unfold.*

Relationship management

The capacity to build and maintain strong, healthy relationships. *This includes communicating clearly, resolving conflict, collaborating effectively and creating space for trust and influence to grow.*

We all want to be seen, heard and understood. Emotional Intelligence is how we offer that — and how we receive it, too.

Emotional Intelligence In Action

Emotional intelligence rarely announces itself — but it often shapes the outcome.

You don't see someone exercising self-restraint, yet you feel the benefit of their composure.

It's the pause that prevents a misstep.
The tone that diffuses tension.
The question that invites a more honest answer.
The presence that helps others feel safe enough to speak up.

Like many soft skills, emotional intelligence isn't always front of mind — especially when things get busy or pressure's high. That's when we tend to default to habit: rushing, withdrawing or reacting.
But the real power of EI shows up in these moments — and it's not always instinctive.

In fact, heightened emotional intelligence often runs counter to what we feel like doing.
It asks us to pause when we feel urgency. To stay open when we want to shut down.
To listen — when everything in us wants to be heard first.

And it's in those moments that emotional intelligence shifts how things unfold:
- Saying less so the conversation doesn't go sideways
- Picking up on what wasn't said
- Staying grounded when someone else isn't
- Leaving space instead of filling it with advice
- Bringing calm presence that creates space for honesty, not fear

These moments are easy to miss — especially when deadlines loom or emotions run high.
But they often leave the deepest impression.

Emotional intelligence doesn't demand attention.
It earns trust — quietly, consistently
and often without a word.

The Pause That Changes Everything

Emotional intelligence involves awareness, but awareness matters most in the moment it affects behavior. That pause is where we stop running on autopilot and start choosing how to think, speak or act.

In that pause, ask:

What am I feeling?

What story am I telling myself?

What response would serve this moment well?

Sometimes that pause prevents tension.

Sometimes it helps you notice the need beneath the words

It may help you hold back a reaction that would not help.

It may help you offer reassurance, encouragement or support.

It may help you listen more closely, show appreciation or notice what someone else needs.

That quick check helps you respond with greater intention.

It helps you bring calm when things feel tense.

It helps you bring warmth when someone needs support.

It helps you respond with more awareness and fewer assumptions.

The pause may be brief.

But it can protect trust, deepen connection and change what happens next.

That is emotional intelligence in action.

> **In a very real sense, we have two minds, one that thinks and one that feels.**

Daniel Goleman

Reflection

- *How easy is it for you to read another person - to get a feel for what they are thinking without their having to tell you? Think about what you notice first.*

- *When stress hits, what do you think a healthy response looks like?*

- *Can you think of someone who's great at reading a room? What do you notice about how they carry themselves and respond to others? What's their demeanor when things get tense?*

Emotional Intelligence in Action

In the heat of the moment, take a breath—stop playing defense, separate facts from your story and choose timing and words that move to a resolution, not a win.

PART TWO

Core Soft Skills
to
Master

- Effective Communication

- Teamwork and Collaboration

- Leadership and Influence

- Adaptability and Flexibility

- Time Management and Organization

Chapter Three

Effective Communication

- Verbal and Nonverbal Communication

- Active Listening Techniques

- The Art of Persuasion and Negotiation

Effective Communication

Communication is where it all comes to life.

Every insight. Every relationship. Every result. This is where soft skills
shift from theory to action — and from intention to real-world impact.

Because no matter how thoughtful someone is — if they can't
communicate it clearly, it gets lost.
Misunderstandings build. Trust frays. Momentum stalls.

But when communication is intentional and clear — things move.
Ideas land. Conversations build clarity instead of confusion.
People feel seen, heard and willing to engage.

Effective communication isn't just about choosing the right words.
It's about choosing the right approach — for the moment, the message
and the person on the other end.

_In this chapter, we'll break down three essential skills that turn
communication into connection:_

- **Verbal and Nonverbal Communication** — _aligning your message
  and your presence to build trust_

- **Active Listening Techniques** — _listening in a way that deepens
  connection and understanding_

- **The Art of Persuasion and Negotiation** — _guiding conversations
  toward shared outcomes_

_**Strong communication isn't "just" a soft skill.
It's the skill that makes all the others work — in
real time, with real people, under real pressure.**_

Verbal and Nonverbal Communication

We've all had times where we thought we were being clear — but the message didn't land.

Because communication isn't just about words.

It's how they're delivered — and how they're received.

Verbal communication includes both spoken and written language.

Tone, pacing and clarity matter just as much in an email as they do in a conversation.
- A calm tone builds trust.
- Pacing gives your message room to land.
- Clarity keeps people focused, not confused.

Nonverbal communication includes facial expressions, gestures, posture, eye contact — even silence. These unspoken cues often carry more weight than words.

Nonverbal communication — including tone — often overrides your words. It can create conflict when your body language, expression or tone send a different message than your words — or it can amplify trust and connection when they align. Either way, that's often all the other person hears.

Mismatch breeds doubt. Alignment builds trust.

Clarity and connection happen when what you say matches what you do.

What It Looks Like in Practice
- Checking your tone before speaking
- Softening your posture for tough feedback
- Holding eye contact when it's hard
- Making sure your facial expressions match your message

Active Listening Techniques

We've all experienced it — talking to someone who's physically present but clearly somewhere else.

They're nodding, maybe making eye contact — but you can tell they've already moved on.

That's the difference between hearing and active listening.

Active listening means being fully present — not just with your ears, but with your attention, body language and intent. It's about tuning into what's being said and...what's underneath it.

Great listeners aren't just staying quiet until it's their turn to talk. They're tuned in — listening to understand, not just respond.

What makes someone a great listener usually isn't complicated. It's small, consistent habits:
- Putting distractions aside
- Letting others finish
- Using quiet cues to show engagement and presence
  They create space — not just for words, but for trust.

That space builds psychological safety — the kind that encourages honesty, ideas and even disagreement without fear.

People speak up more when they don't feel like they're being judged or rushed.

And the more present you are, the safer they feel.

Done well, active listening transforms communication from a transaction into a connection.

What It Looks Like in Practice
- Silencing your phone and making eye contact
- Letting the other person finish before replying
- Reflecting back what you heard before offering advice
- Staying engaged and curious ~ asking follow-up questions

The Art of Persuasion and Negotiation

Persuasion and negotiation aren't about getting your way.

They're about guiding conversations toward outcomes that work —
for everyone involved.

And yet many people treat them like a zero-sum game of win or lose.
That's when trust breaks down and collaboration stalls.

Pressure shuts people down. Power plays create quiet pushback.
True persuasion is about clarity and connection — not control.

You use it more than you think:
- Leading a meeting
- Asking for support
- Offering feedback
- Working through conflict

The goal isn't to dominate — it's to earn buy-in.
Buy-in is what inspires people to go beyond the bare minimum.

You've probably done it yourself — stayed late or stepped in to
help — not because you had to, but because you wanted to. That's
discretionary effort and it only shows up when people feel included
and respected. You can't demand it. But you can create the conditions
for it.

This becomes an art when you sense where people are, meet them
there and move the conversation forward with confidence and care.

The most persuasive people don't push. They listen. They frame things
clearly. They adjust their tone. They know timing and presence matter
just as much as the message.

What It Looks Like in Practice

- Reflecting back on what you heard before offering a solution
- Naming shared goals to build alignment
- Shifting tone when energy changes and remaining calm
- Asking open-ended questions to uncover what matters most

Make Every Message Land

Communication often fails when one person holds an expectation the other never agreed to.

A simple but powerful distinction:

An **expectation** is what one person assumes.
An **agreement** is what both people confirm.

Always take one extra step to confirm who will do what, by when and what success looks like.

That small step turns expectations into agreements and clarity into accountability.

Expectation:
"I assumed you were taking care of that."

Agreement:
"You'll send the final numbers by 3 and I'll submit the report by 4. Does that work?"

Confirmation:
"Yes. I'll send the final numbers by 3."

Clear communication does not end with what's said.
It ends with what's confirmed.

Habits that Multiply Clarity

The 3 W's ~ for Crystal Clear Communication

In under 60 seconds, answer 3 questions;

- **Why:** Why this matters
- **What**: What you need
- **When**: When you need it and what you'll do next

Example ~ Sender
Why: Weekly report needs final numbers for accuracy.
What: Please add the updated revenue line.
When: I will send the report at 4 p.m. once yours is in.

Example ~ Receiver
Got it — I'll add the revenue line by 3 p.m. and ping you when it's done.

Active Listening ~ the 30-second check

Hear. Mirror. Confirm. Act.

One line back: "What I hear is _______. Did I get that right?"

- Use their exact nouns and numbers
- Ask one clean question
- Close with your next step in one line

Example ~ Listener
"What I hear is you want draft #2 with the new chart by noon. I'll send it by 11:45. Did I get that right?"

You can have the most brilliant ideas, but if you can't get them across, your ideas won't get you anywhere.

Lee Iacocca

Reflection

- *Why do you think the right words can sometimes land the wrong way?*

- *When you are on the listening side, do you find yourself more often trying to hear their point or waiting for a break in the conversation to make yours?*

- *Can you recall a time when you went above and beyond what was expected for a cause or project? What made you feel compelled to step up? How did your contribution make you feel afterwards?*

Effective Communication in Action

When delivering instructions, rather than just expecting that they are understood, get agreement that they are both understood and will be carried out as directed. Recognize the difference between 'expectation' and 'agreement'. Expectation is an assumption and agreement is a commitment.

Chapter Four

Teamwork and Collaboration

- Building and Maintaining Trust in Teams

- The Importance of Being Nonjudgmental

- Conflict and Resolution

Teamwork and Collaboration

Great teams don't just happen — they're built in small, everyday moments.

When a team works, you can feel it.
Trust builds. People step up. Ideas get better.
And even when challenges come up — people stay committed.

But when a team breaks down, the damage adds up fast.
Tension builds. Trust drops. People go quiet — collaboration stalls.

No matter how skilled or smart someone is, their ability to collaborate shapes the results, the relationships and the culture.

Researcher Amy Edmondson calls it psychological safety — a shared belief that it's safe to speak up, take risks and be yourself without fear of embarrassment or punishment.

It's not about being soft. It's about creating an environment where people can contribute freely — and that matters for everyone, not just leaders.

You don't have to be best friends to be a strong team.
But you do have to show up with respect, consistency and a willingness to engage.

In this chapter, we'll look at three essential elements of real teamwork:

- **Building and Maintaining Trust** — *the foundation for every healthy team dynamic*

- **The Importance of Being Non-Judgmental** — *creating space where people feel safe and seen*

- **Conflict and Resolution** — *handling tension in a way that leads to clarity, not chaos*

Building and Maintaining Trust in Teams

When trust is strong, teams work better — plain and simple.

People offer ideas, take ownership and support each other.
They solve problems faster, stay engaged and adapt when plans shift.

But when trust is missing, everything slows down.
People hold back. Decisions stall. Morale dips.

Even the smartest teams can get stuck — not because they lack talent, but because they can't talk openly if collaboration and psychological safety aren't there.

When that happens, the cost is real: good people disengage, deadlines slip and the company pays for it in turnover, lost momentum and money.

The good news? Trust isn't magic — it's built in moments.
It grows through consistency, honesty and follow-through.
It builds when people own their mistakes, welcome feedback and keep their word — even when it's inconvenient.

When trust becomes the norm, everything gets easier — conversations, decisions and progress. You become someone others rely on, respect and want to work with.

It's the consistent actions that tell people: You can count on me.
That's what builds trust — and keeps it strong.

What It Looks Like in Practice

- Following through without being chased
- Admitting mistakes and taking responsibility
- Speaking honestly, without harshness
- Showing up on time

The Importance of Being Non-Judgemental

We all like to believe we're fair-minded.

But the truth is — we all carry bias.
Some of it's learned. Some of it's unconscious.

And if we're not careful, it can shape how we treat people — often without realizing it.

That's why suspending judgment to stay open is so powerful.

Being nonjudgmental doesn't mean lowering your standards.
It means staying open — and aware of how quickly our brains make assumptions.

When people feel judged, they shut down.
They question their value. They second-guess their contributions.
They worry more about their image than their ability.

However, when people feel truly safe, they contribute more.
That's psychological safety in action.
It encourages people to show up fully — to think out loud,
challenge ideas and bring their whole self to the work.

And it's something anyone on a team can help create.

But keeping that space alive takes more than interest — it takes emotional intelligence, self-awareness and the discipline to hold back quick judgments.

That's how trust grows stronger and makes great teams possible.

What It Looks Like in Practice

- Noticing assumptions before they affect your response
- Asking questions before jumping to conclusions
- Giving feedback without tone or shame
- Getting clarity instead of guessing motives

Conflict and Resolution

When people work closely together, conflict is inevitable.

We all bring different pressures, perspectives and priorities to the table.

Conflict isn't the problem.
Avoiding it — or mishandling it — is.

Unresolved conflict wears people down.
It creates tension that lingers — even after the conversation ends.
It keeps people guarded — less open, less willing to engage.

But when handled constructively, conflict strengthens a team by clearing the air, resolving what's been holding people back and replacing tension with understanding and respect.

That only happens when people feel heard — and know how to stay grounded in tough moments.

That's where emotional intelligence shows up.
It doesn't mean you agree with everything.

It means you stay present, listen without judgment and respond without attacking or withdrawing.

You can be direct and still be respectful. You can disagree and keep trust intact.

Handled well, conflict becomes a path to clarity, not division.

That starts with listening fully, focusing on the issue — not the person — and aiming for a solution everyone can stand behind.

What It Looks Like in Practice

- Pressing pause when tension rises
- Naming what's really going on
- Listening without interrupting or defending
- Focusing on the resolution more than your being right

> **"It's so much better to be in a workplace where you can be your real self and contribute to the work in a meaningful way."**
>
> Amy Edmondson

Reflection

- *What do you do that shows your teammates they can count on you? What do your teammates do that shows you they've got your back? How would you describe that give and take?*

- *When someone on your team drops the ball, what's your first reaction?*

- *How do you handle differing viewpoints with your teammates?*

Teamwork and Collaboration in Action

When presenting a challenge, include possible solutions to show that you are invested in the team's success. It demonstrates you did the thinking and care about outcomes.

Chapter Five

Leadership and Influence

- Leading with Empathy and Compassion

- Motivating and Inspiring Others

- Decision-Making and Problem-Solving

Leadership and Influence

Strong leadership sets the tone for everything — trust, momentum and culture.

It's about how you show up, how you treat people and how you help the team move forward — especially when things get tough.

Some of the most impactful leaders step up in the moment — not because of their title, but because they lead with calm, clarity and initiative when it counts.

Researchers like Daniel Goleman and Brené Brown have shown that emotional intelligence — self-awareness, empathy and trust-building — directly impacts performance, engagement and retention.

Their work reinforces what great leaders already know: when people feel seen, safe and supported, they show up stronger.

And you don't need a title to lead this way — influence comes from presence, not position.

This chapter looks at three essential skills that help you stay steady, adapt quickly and lead well under pressure:

- **Leading with Empathy and Compassion** — _how understanding people's needs and emotions builds connection and trust_

- **Motivating and Inspiring Others** — _how to spark enthusiasm, encourage growth and bring out the best in ourselves_

- **Decision-Making and Problem Solving** — _how to weigh options, stay steady under pressure and drive smart, practical solutions_

**_The real power of leadership isn't in authority —
it's in influence._**

Leading with Empathy and Compassion

Every leader wants their team to perform — but performance isn't driven by pressure alone.

It's fueled by trust, connection and the sense that you're understood.

People don't just respond to authority — they respond to how they're treated.
They give more when they feel seen, supported and respected.

But in fast-paced environments, empathy often takes a back seat to deadlines.
That's when teams start to shut down, disengage or burn out.

Empathy isn't about being soft. It's about paying attention — understanding what people need to stay steady and focused.
Unlike ***sympathy***, which often feels distant or pitying, empathy means getting closer.
It's about tuning in — not fixing, not judging — just seeing someone clearly in their moment.

That's what creates connection. When people feel safe and seen, they open up. They speak honestly. They trust your lead. That trust holds teams together under pressure.

Compassion brings in humanity. It builds loyalty, fuels resilience and drives performance.

You don't need a title to lead this way. When you listen and care, people trust you and work better with you.

What It Looks Like in Practice

- Listening to understand, not just respond
- Checking in before checking tasks
- Giving feedback with care, not criticism
- Offering support when someone is under pressure

Motivating and Inspiring Others

Everyone wants to feel energized, valued and connected to work that matters — and to know that their contribution makes a difference.

When teams are aligned — with a clear goal and shared momentum — things move. Energy rises. Ideas build.

People go the extra mile — not because they have to, but because they want to.

But that energy fades when connection breaks — between teammates, between roles or between the work and the why. Motivation dips. Momentum stalls. People disengage — not from apathy, but from misalignment.

That's not just a morale problem. It's a performance one.

Strong leaders don't just give direction — they create connection. They help people feel part of something bigger — and remind them why it matters.

Motivation comes from clarity, recognition and shared purpose — not pressure or pep talks.

That happens when leaders notice what's working, name strengths out loud and link everyday effort to the bigger picture.

Inspiration spreads through trust, encouragement and steady presence.

People don't just follow instructions — they respond to presence. And one person's energy can lift the whole team.

What It Looks Like in Practice
- Sharing specific praise for effort and progress
- Reconnecting the team to purpose when morale dips
- Reinforcing team strengths during pressure or change
- Being present, a team player and walking your talk

Decision-Making and Problem-Solving

In high-pressure moments, it's easy to react fast and regret it later.

That's when people skip steps, miss key info or jump to fixes that don't solve the real problem. The cost? Wasted time. Missteps. Damaged trust.

In tough situations, how you think matters as much as what you do.

Strong decision-making starts with clarity.
Smart problem-solving begins by slowing down and asking: What's really going on — and what outcome matters most?

When pressure rises, people look for steady minds and calm presence.

You don't need all the answers. But you do need to stay grounded, ask better questions and resist the urge to move too fast.

It's less about control and more about composure and clarity.
That kind of thinking starts with curiosity.

By listening first, inviting input and mapping the real issue — not just the symptoms — you create smarter strategies.

It's not overthinking. It's intentional thinking.

People trust those who pause, assess and take things seriously — especially under stress. Clear thinking leads to better results.

When you take time to understand the real issue, invite perspective and stay focused on what matters most — you make more effective decisions and earn deeper trust.

What It Looks Like in Practice
- Pausing to assess before reacting
- Asking "What are we really working to solve here?"
- Weighing the options before committing
- Taking time to reflect and think clearly before making a decision

"Leadership is influence — nothing more, nothing less.

John C. Maxwell

Reflection

- *Who comes to mind when you think of someone who led with clarity and created an environment where you felt safe to speak up and encouraged to contribute?*

- *How do you take part in motivating your team's performance? (Backing a new initiative, offering help to a colleague or sharing research and valuable insights? How do you contribute as a team player?*

- *When challenges arise, what's your next move after that first moment of awareness? Do you pause instead of reacting too soon? How do you get the clarity you need to move forward wisely?*

Leadership and Influence in Action

When confusion shows up, you own it. You realign the team and verify what each person heard and will do next. Taking ownership demonstrates leadership—protecting time, budget and morale.

Chapter Six

Adaptability and Flexibility

- Embracing Change and Uncertainty

- Cultivating a Growth Mindset

- Balancing Work and Personal Life

Adaptability and Flexibility

Change isn't always optional.

Shifting priorities, new technologies, unexpected challenges — today's work environment moves fast. And when people can't adapt, they fall behind.

Stress builds. Resistance kicks in.
Energy goes toward holding on — instead of moving forward.

Adaptability isn't about liking change.
It's about staying flexible, focused and resilient — even when things feel uncertain or uncomfortable.

Whether you're navigating change or leading others through it, this chapter gives you tools to stay grounded and intentional — even when the path forward is unclear.

We'll look at three key skills that help you stay steady , adjust quickly and keep growing through it all:

- **Embracing Change and Uncertainty** — _handling the unknown with less frustration and more perspective_

- **Cultivating a Growth Mindset** — _how to stay curious, build confidence and keep learning from every experience_

- **Balancing Work and Personal Life** — _adjusting your energy and focus to match what matters most_

Embracing Change and Uncertainty

Change can be uncomfortable — especially when it's unexpected or outside your control.

It's natural to crave stability. But in today's workplace, change is constant — and resisting it only makes it harder.

You don't have to love change to get better at facing it.
Just meet it with less resistance and more openness.

Uncertainty is often the hardest part.
Not knowing how things will play out triggers stress and doubt.
But staying grounded — even when the path isn't clear — builds real resilience.

One way to meet change with more steadiness:
- Pause before reacting — even if you feel resistant
- Ask questions instead of jumping to conclusions
- Focus on what you can control
- Give the change a chance before writing it off

Embracing change doesn't mean faking enthusiasm.

It means shifting from frustration to curiosity — and staying open to the idea that something good might come from it.

That might look like:
- Rolling with a process change — not rolling your eyes
- Adjusting to a new manager's style
- Staying flexible during a reorg

How you show up in these moments shapes how others see you — and how well you move forward.

People who stay steady in change tend to get noticed — not just for their attitude, but for their impact.

What It Looks Like in Practice
- Adjusting calmly to a new system or policy
- Staying open to feedback when roles shift
- Helping others adapt instead of adding stress
- Allowing curiosity to preempt resistance

Cultivating a Growth Mindset

Growth happens when we stay open, curious and willing to learn.

It stalls when we resist something new — "just" because it's new.

A closed mindset shows up when people avoid challenges, resist feedback or believe that struggling means they've failed.

The cost is real.
Progress slows. Morale dips. People play defense instead of leaning into potential.

Even high performers fall into a fixed mindset now and then.

A growth mindset changes that.

Psychologist Carol Dweck's research popularized the idea of a growth mindset — the belief that skills and intelligence can be developed through effort and feedback.

That belief shifts the focus from fear of failure to steady improvement — especially when things get hard.

In fast-moving workplaces, this mindset helps people stay resilient, coachable and curious.

Instead of shutting down — they keep learning, lead by example and try again with new insight.

The shift is simple: be curious, try new approaches and aim for progress.

Over time, this fuels confidence, trust and a culture where growth is expected — and supported.

What It Looks Like in Practice
- Reworking a plan based on what didn't work
- Encouraging someone else's effort to improve
- Seeing challenges as a chance to lean in — not opt out
- Focusing on progress as opposed to perfection

Balancing Work and Personal Life

Most people treat balance like a time problem — trying to squeeze more into less. But the real issue is misalignment.

A fulfilling life isn't just built at work — or outside of it.
It's shaped by the balance between both.

When that rhythm feels right, work feels more purposeful — and life feels more present. But when the balance is off, even the smallest tasks can start to feel heavy. That's when stress builds, motivation dips and people start to disconnect — from both their goals and joy.

Work-life balance doesn't mean splitting time evenly.

It means being present in your responsibilities while still feeling connected to the rest of your life.

Real balance starts with clarity.
When you know what kind of life you're building — not someday, but now — every decision gets easier.
You know when you're on track. And when you're not.

You create balance by making small, intentional choices — consistently:
- Define what outcomes you want — not just at work, but in life
- Say no to what's off track — yes to what moves you forward
- Protect time for relationships and health

Staying balanced doesn't mean you'll never feel overwhelmed.

It means you'll recognize the signs early — and know how to reset before it takes a bigger toll.

What It Looks Like in Practice
- Blocking off time for focused work and true rest
- Setting boundaries around email, messages or late-night tasks
- Recognizing signs of stress - asking for help before you burn out
- Scheduling interests or activities outside of work

**"You don't know
what your abilities
are until you make a
full commitment to
developing them."**

Carol Dweck

Reflection

- *When plans change - what gets you back to curious and flexible?*

- *Do you tend to be receptive and curious with new people or do you find yourself more often forming an opinion about them quickly?*

- *How well do you balance caring for your health and life outside of work? Do you give it the same energy you give to meeting deadlines and expectations at work? Where do you fit "You" into your day?*

Adaptability and Flexibility in Action

Understanding that a new team leader will have a different style and working to understand and support them rather than fighting the change. Demonstrates professionalism and maturity while reducing friction and rework while the leader learns the team.

Chapter Seven

Time Management and Organization

- Prioritizing Tasks and Managing Deadlines

- Overcoming Procrastination

- Techniques for Staying Organized and Focused

Time Management and Organization

Time management isn't about squeezing more into your day — it's about focusing your time where it counts.

Being human comes with distractions, shifting priorities and unexpected curveballs.

If you're not focused, it's easy to feel like the day is running you — not the other way around.

Even strong systems benefit from small refinements — steady habits that sharpen focus, restore energy and bring more clarity to your day.

The goal isn't doing it all.
It's doing the right things — at the right time — in a way that supports your focus, follow-through and performance.

In this chapter, we'll explore three core practices that help make that possible:

- **Prioritizing Tasks and Managing Deadlines** — _figuring out what matters most without burning out_

- **Overcoming Procrastination** — _breaking the stall cycle and building momentum_

- **Techniques for Staying Organized and Focused** — _clearing the noise and following through_

Working with your time — instead of reacting to it — helps you stay clear, consistent and effective when it counts.

Prioritizing Tasks and Managing Deadlines

When your priorities are clear, your day feels different.

You focus more. You stress less. And you move through your work with a greater sense of purpose and progress — not just pressure.

But without that clarity? Every task starts to feel urgent. Everything feels important. And that's when overwhelm kicks in.

Prioritizing isn't just about making a list. It's about knowing what moves things forward — and what can wait. It's sorting the essential from the noise so you can give your best effort where it matters most.

Managing deadlines helps anchor that focus.

Clear timelines give structure and direction. But even the best calendar won't help if the priorities underneath it aren't aligned.

You can create that alignment by asking yourself:
- What's urgent — and what's just loud?
- What will have the biggest impact today?
- What would make everything else easier if I did it first?

Plans shift. But clarity helps you adjust without losing momentum.

Pausing to check in — instead of rushing through — helps you make better decisions about where your time and energy go.

Over time, those small moments of clarity lead to bigger results.

The more often you pause to prioritize, the more progress you'll make — with less stress.

What It Looks Like in Practice
- Choosing one clear focus at the start of your day
- Breaking large projects into smaller, deadline-driven steps
- Blocking time for high-impact tasks — and sticking to it
- Identifying the low-priority tasks and scheduling accordingly

Overcoming Procrastination

You know what needs to get done — but you hesitate.
Delay turns into pressure. The task feels heavier.

It's easy to mistake that for laziness. It's not.

Procrastination is often a signal — something's in the way.
As organizational psychologist Adam Grant puts it:
"Procrastination is not a time management problem. It's an emotion management problem."

Maybe the task feels overwhelming.
Maybe you're unsure where to start.
Maybe doubt is creeping in — or you're simply drained.

Everyone procrastinates now and then.
The key is noticing it — and shifting with intention.
The first step isn't about willpower.
It's about clarity.

Ask: What exactly am I avoiding — and why?
That pause breaks the cycle.
Once you name the barrier, you can move with purpose — not pressure.

Don't wait for the perfect moment. Just start.
The smallest action builds momentum.
Progress isn't about perfection.
It's about movement.

And once you're in motion, the weight of avoidance starts to lift.

What It Looks Like in Practice

- Breaking a task into smaller steps— and starting from there
- Setting a timer for 10 minutes of focused effort
- Choosing one thing to finish instead of juggling too much
- When avoiding something ~ question yourself to know why

Techniques for Staying Organized and Focused

When you're organized and focused, work feels smoother —
and your brain feels lighter.

You move through the day with more purpose, fewer mistakes and
less stress.

But when your attention is scattered?
You may still be working hard — but it's tougher to see progress.

Without focus, it's easy to bounce between tasks, react to every ping
and finish the day feeling busy but not productive.

Staying organized is about keeping things manageable, even when
plans change.
It's about building small habits that keep you steady and on track —
especially when distractions are constant.

That includes how you structure your space, protect your priorities
and regroup when things start to slip.

You can support better focus by making a few intentional shifts:
- Start your day by identifying your top three priorities
- Block off time for deep work — even 25 minutes can help
- Clear the clutter — from your workspace, inbox and browser tabs
- Use simple tools or cues that help you refocus quickly

These habits do more than keep things tidy — they help you follow
through, reduce stress and stay present for what matters.

What It Looks Like in Practice

- Using a simple system to track your to-dos and deadlines
- Resetting or clearing your space at the end of each day
- Taking short breaks to recharge your energy and clarity
- Turning off 'notifications' to avoid distractions

Procrastination is not a time management problem. It's an emotion management problem.

Adam Grant

Reflection

- *What's your go-to system for making sure you meet your deadlines, goals and everyday responsibilities? Do you find yourself focusing on more important or urgent items?*

- *When you find yourself procrastinating - do you take a step back and question what's really behind the avoidance?*

- *Would you consider yourself organized? If yes, what do you credit it to? If not, what small habits could help you feel more in control and on top of things?*

Time Management and Organization in Action

You have a clear 3–5 year picture of where you want to be, so you know if your day-to-day actions move you closer or further from your outcome. That focus helps you schedule with intent and prioritize progress over busyness.

PART THREE

EMOTIONAL INTELLIGENCE AND HOW IT SUPPORTS SOFT SKILLS

Chapter Eight

Self Awareness
and
Self Regulation

- Identifying and Understanding Your Emotions

- Managing Stress and Emotional Reactions

- Developing Resilience and Emotional Stability

Self-Awareness and Self-Regulation

Understanding yourself is one of the most valuable skills you can develop — and it starts with emotional awareness.

When you can name what you're feeling, stay steady under pressure and bounce back from challenges, you build more than confidence — you build trust, clarity and resilience.

This chapter looks at three foundational skills that help you lead yourself well, even in tough moments:

- **Identifying and Understanding Your Emotions** — *how recognizing what you're feeling (and why) helps you pause, process and respond intentionally*

- **Managing Stress and Emotional Reactions** — *how to handle pressure and triggers in a healthy, productive way that keeps communication clear and relationships strong*

- **Developing Resilience and Emotional Stability** — *how to build the flexibility and steadiness to bounce back from setbacks, stay focused and inspire confidence*

Identifying and Understanding Your Emotions

Emotions move fast.
They can shift in an instant — triggered by a thought, a tone, a glance.

Loud or subtle, they show up in how you think, speak and interact.
They shape your tone, timing and body language — all of which affect how your message lands.

If you miss the early signs of stress or frustration, emotion takes over — and good intentions get lost.

That's why emotional awareness matters.

Organizational psychologist Tasha Eurich found that while 95% of people believe they're self-aware, only about 10–15% actually are.
That gap affects everything from performance to trust.

Emotional awareness is the ability to notice when something feels off — especially when your reaction seems bigger than the moment.

Those cues are worth paying attention to.
It gives you space to pause — so your response reflects your purpose, not just your mood.
Even positive emotions like excitement or pride can throw you off if you're not tuned in.

Self-awareness helps steady your internal tone — so your external one lands with clarity and respect.
It's how you lead with your values, not just your emotions.

What It Looks Like in Practice

- Naming what you're feeling instead of brushing it off
- Catching shifts in your tone or energy before speaking
- Letting your values shape your words — not just your emotions
- When feeling stressed ~ question what's really driving the stress

Managing Stress and Emotional Reactions

Stress is unavoidable — but how you respond to it makes all the difference.

As we highlighted earlier, in high-pressure moments, emotional steadiness isn't just helpful — it's a leadership skill.

It brings calm to tense situations and helps others stay focused, as people tend to take emotional cues from whoever is calmest in the room.

But when stress takes over, reactions get sharper — and communication suffers. Even brilliant, well-meaning people can say or do things they regret when emotions start to run the show.

Managing emotional reactions isn't about pretending everything's fine. It's about staying aware of your internal state — and building the skills to pause, regulate and respond with intention.

That starts with small shifts:
- Notice when your body tightens or your tone changes
- Use breath, movement or a short break to reset
- Pause before responding in emotionally charged moments

This isn't about controlling emotions. It's about being able to move through them — instead of being controlled by them.

That steadiness builds more than resilience. It earns trust. It improves communication. And it helps create environments where people feel safe, respected and able to think clearly — even under stress.

What It Looks Like in Practice
- Noticing rising frustration and stepping away before reacting
- Delivering hard feedback with focused calm and clarity
- Taking a moment before replying to a tense or intense message
- Knowing when it's time to step back and take deep breaths

Developing Resilience and Emotional Stability

Resilience isn't something you're born with.

It's a capability — built through self-awareness, recovery and small, **intentional habits** that keep you grounded through stress and change.

When resilience is strong, pressure doesn't rattle you. You think more clearly, adapt faster and support others without absorbing their stress.

It also helps you stay emotionally steady — so you're less likely to get flustered, reactive or thrown off course.

But without that stability, even small setbacks can feel overwhelming.
Focus slips. Emotions spike.
Burnout builds quietly — until it doesn't.

Every time you pause to reset — whether that means taking a breath, stepping away or tackling one thing at a time — you strengthen your ability to think clearly and stay steady under pressure.

The more often you practice it, the more it becomes your default.

That includes recharging when your energy dips, focusing on what you can control, choosing progress over perfect, creating routines that restore calm and viewing setbacks as part of growth.

These habits don't just help you bounce back — they help you stay ready. Ready to lead, adapt and stay present under pressure.

Because grounded people listen better, speak more clearly and lead with steadiness — not stress.

What It Looks Like in Practice

- Returning to priorities when the day gets off track
- Responding with flexibility when plans shift
- Journaling or debriefing to gain clarity after hard moments
- Knowing what recharges your energy and making time for it

Reflection

- *In real time - when you are stressed or frustrated, do you notice it in your body or your thoughts first? What helps you respond well?*

- *What do people around you pick up on when you're under stress?*

- *When you face a setback, after your initial disappointment, how open are you to treating it as an opportunity for growth?*

Self-Awareness and Self-Regulation in Action

You notice new information puts you on edge. You pause, name the feeling, take a slow breath and reset so you can respond with clarity, not react from stress. Regulating your state models psychological safety for the team.

Chapter Nine

Empathy and Social Awareness

- Reading People and the Room

- Building Strong Interpersonal Relationships

- The Role of Empathy in Conflict Resolution

Empathy and Social Awareness

These quiet strengths transform how we connect, communicate and collaborate.

At their core, they're about recognizing and understanding the feelings, perspectives and needs of others — making people feel seen, heard and respected.

Social awareness also means staying mindful of cultural differences and being open to how others might communicate, express emotion or interpret tone.

Without that awareness, even well-intended communication can fall flat — or cause unintended disconnect.

In this chapter, we'll explore three ways to strengthen the relationships that shape how others experience and trust you:

- **Reading People and the Room** — _tuning in, listening without judgment and being fully present to bring out the best in others_

- **Building Strong Interpersonal Relationships** — _how everyday interactions shape credibility, influence and well-being and why they're worth protecting_

- **The Role of Empathy in Conflict Resolution** — _how empathy defuses tension, opens dialogue and turns conflict into collaboration_

Reading People and the Room

Empathy and social awareness don't always get noticed or talked about — but they play a key (often hidden) role in building strong relationships and successful teams.

They help people feel seen, heard and respected. They shape how trust is built, how conflict is handled and how communication lands.

Without them? Even good intentions can misfire. We miss cues. We talk past each other. Trust takes a hit — not out of carelessness, but because we weren't paying attention.

Empathy is understanding what someone else is feeling — even when they don't say it. It's reading a person or the room.
Social awarenesss is sensing what's beneath the surface — reading the person and the room — and adjusting your behavior with care.

They're essential soft skills, showing up in moments like:
- Sensing when someone's overwhelmed — and helping out
- Holding back advice and just listening
- Picking up on tension before it turns into conflict.
- Adjusting your tone to fit the moment, not your mood

You don't have to absorb every emotion or agree with every view. But staying present and respectful — especially when stakes are high — is what the best communicators and leaders do.

Empathy and social awareness don't just make you more considerate — they make conversations smoother, problems easier to solve and trust quicker to build.

Respect lowers defensiveness, which speeds clarity to solutions.

What It Looks Like in Practice
- Pausing to read body language before responding
- Listening without interrupting or rushing to solve
- Asking how someone's doing instead of assuming
- Being aware of your tone - in both your voice and body language

Building Strong Interpersonal Relationships

Strong relationships are the foundation of trust, teamwork and influence.

They make conversations easier, decisions faster and tough moments more manageable.

And when they're missing?
Communication breaks down — Tensions build.
Even simple tasks start to feel harder than they need to be.

That's why interpersonal relationships aren't just nice to have — they're essential to how we work, lead and collaborate.

They shape how much people trust you, how openly they communicate and how willing they are to follow your lead.

Trust builds in what we do consistently — following through, listening without distraction, checking in, giving credit and showing up when it counts.

It's not about being everyone's best friend.
It's about helping people feel respected, seen and safe.

At the core, we all want to be respected and understood — regardless of our title.

The stronger your relationships, the more effective your communication — and the easier it becomes to navigate tension, build alignment and move through conflict with clarity.

What It Looks Like in Practice

- Remembering personal details that show people they matter
- Making time for others — even when you're busy
- Following through on what you said you'd do
- Giving genuine praise when it's due

The Role of Empathy in Conflict Resolution

Conflict is inevitable.

Different goals, experiences or communication styles naturally create tension. That's not failure — that's difference.

Handled well, conflict leads to clarity, alignment and stronger results. Handled poorly, it breeds resentment and distrust.

Empathy tips the balance. By recognizing what someone else is feeling — and responding with care instead of blame — space is created for understanding, even in disagreement.

When people feel heard, they stop fighting to be heard.
The energy shifts. Reactions slow. That's when space opens to hear what's really behind the words — frustration, fear, uncertainty.

Empathy helps shift the response from control to curiosity.
It doesn't mean giving in. It means showing their experience matters — and that the goal is to move forward, not just prove a point.

Even small moves make a difference: a pause before responding, a simple "I hear that."

Empathy doesn't erase conflict. But it keeps it from becoming destructive. It opens the door to resolution, preserves dignity and builds trust — in the moment and long after.

Because in the end, people remember less about the conflict itself— and more about the respect and care they experienced.

What It Looks Like in Practice

- Pausing before reacting to give space for clarity
- Asking, "What would a good outcome look like to you?"
- Staying calm and respectful when conversations get tense
- Taking into consideration what the other is thinking

I've learned that people will forget what you said, people will forget what you did, but people will never forget how you made them feel.

Maya Angelou

Reflection

- *Have you ever softened or shifted your words because you understood where the other person was coming from?*

- *How do you think the other person knows when you are truly listening? What do you think is their first clue that you are being present and engaged for them?*

- *Can you think of a time when mutual trust sped up a process because everyone was aligned?*

Empathy and Social Awareness in Action

Acknowledge a mistake and take ownership with a plan to correct. Allow others the same space you would want when they make a mistake. This lowers defensiveness so problems surface sooner.

Chapter Ten

Building and Maintaining Relationships

- Effective Networking Strategies

- Strengthening Personal Relationships

- The Importance of Trust and Respect

Building and Maintaining Relationships

At the heart of personal and professional success lies one essential skill: the ability to build and maintain meaningful relationships.

They shape how people see us, how much they trust us — and whether they want to work with us, support us or follow our lead.

Strong relationships don't happen by accident.

They're built through small, consistent actions — and when they're in place, everything else works better.

This chapter highlights three key ways to build and strengthen the relationships that make everything else work:

- **Effective Networking Strategies** — *how to connect with purpose, listen with intention and offer value without expectation*

- **Strengthening Personal and Professional Connections** — *how to build bonds that last through consistency, presence and care*

- **The Importance of Trust and Respect** — *why they're the foundation of influence, collaboration and long-term success*

These skills make relationships stronger, communication clearer and outcomes better — in work, in life and the impact you make.

Effective Networking Strategies

Strong networks aren't built by accident.

They're built through trust, generosity and follow-through — and they become one of your most valuable assets.

Some of the most meaningful opportunities in life and work may start with a handshake or a quick introduction — but they grow through trust, consistency and genuine connection.

When networking is rushed or transactional, it falls flat.
But when it's built on shared values and small, thoughtful actions, it becomes a source of connection, collaboration and support.

Effective networking isn't about knowing everyone.
It's about nurturing the right relationships — the kind where both people feel seen, valued and better for having connected.

You don't need a strategy deck or a polished pitch.
You need a simple habit of showing up with sincerity and staying in touch with intention.

A few small moves make a big impact:
- Reaching out just to check in — not only when needed
- Sharing an article or opportunity they might appreciate
- Introducing people who could benefit knowing each other

These aren't grand gestures.
But over time, they shape the kind of reputation people remember — and relationships that last.

People don't just remember who made the contact — they remember who stayed connected.

What It Looks Like in Practice
- Following up after a brief conversation with a note or resource
- Staying connected with former colleagues or mentors
- Offering help or introductions without expecting reciprocation
- Keeping your word and doing what you say you will

Strengthening Personal and Professional Connections

Strong relationships don't just make work and life more enjoyable — they make them more effective.

Not just in moments of celebration — but especially under pressure, in conflict or when things don't go as planned.

But when demands pile up and urgency takes priority over people, connection quietly fades.

Check-ins get skipped. Tones get sharp. And even solid relationships start to wear down — not from malice, but from neglect.

That's why consistency matters.

The strongest connections are built through presence, follow-through and small moments that show people they matter — especially when there's nothing in it for you.

That can be as simple as:
- Remembering small details heard casually and following up
- Checking in when someone's going through a hard time
- Sharing praise publicly and feedback privately
- Being fully present — not just physically, but emotionally

These gestures don't have to be grand — but they do need to be consistent.

They create a foundation of trust that strengthens collaboration, supports honest dialogue and makes it easier to work through hard things together.

What It Looks Like in Practice
- Following through on small promises — even informal ones
- Giving someone your full attention in a conversation
- Noticing when someone's off — and checking in with them
- Making contact without an agenda - to say "hi ~ hello"

The Importance of Trust and Respect

Trust and respect are the foundation of every strong relationship — personal or professional.

They create a culture where people feel safe to speak up, contribute and show up as themselves. That's when communication flows. Decisions move faster. Accountability rises.

People step up, stretch themselves and stay committed — even when things get hard.

But when trust breaks down or respect feels one-sided, everything slows. People hold back. Motivation drops. Collaboration weakens.

What could've been a small issue snowballs — not because it was big, but because the relationship was already strained.

You don't have to be liked by everyone to earn trust.
But you do need to be steady — consistent in how you show up, fair in how you lead and intentional in how you treat others.

Trust and respect grow through action:
Keeping your word. Giving credit. Owning mistakes. Treating people with dignity — especially in disagreement.

They're not just personal values.
They're performance multipliers.
Because when people trust you and feel respected, they show up stronger, collaborate better and stay engaged.

That's how reputations grow, loyalty deepens and success scales.

What It Looks Like in Practice

- Following through on what you promised — even the small stuff
- Listening with attention — without interrupting or dismissing
- Asking for feedback — and accepting it with humility
- Only making promises you can keep

Being heard is so close to being loved that for the average person, they are almost indistinguishable.

David Augsburger

Reflection

- *Think of someone you trust completely. What is it about them that makes you feel they are trustworthy?*

- *How do you stay connected with the relationships that matter most to you?*

- *How are you at keeping your word? Do you show up when you say you will, follow through on what you promised?*

Building and Maintaining Relationships in Action

You learn of a great connection that would benefit a colleague or friend and you pass it along with no strings or expectations attached. Positions you as a giver not a taker.

PART FOUR

The Integration

- Pulling it All Together

- The Quiet Power

Pulling It All Together

We've touched on key soft skills — and the emotional intelligence that strengthens them.

Some may have felt familiar. Others, new.

But they all point toward the same outcome: better communication, stronger relationships and meaningful growth — for everyone involved.

And that matters.
Because people don't work in isolation.
We work with people. For people. Through people.

And those people want the same things you do — to feel heard, valued and respected.

This book was written to help us all do that better.

Yes, you may already practice many of these skills.
But let's be honest — when pressure hits, it's easy to lose sight of the bigger picture.

This isn't about starting from scratch.
It's about becoming even more aware — so we can lead, connect and communicate with greater intention.

Because the real skill isn't just saying the right thing —
It's showing up in a way that helps others feel safe, seen and motivated to do their best too.

That's where emotional intelligence and soft skills intersect.
Together, they create a communication style that's clear, confident and deeply human.

They help you:
- Stay calm when emotions run high
- Shift gears when plans change
- Lead with steadiness — even in hard moments

Soft skills bring the Platinum Rule to life:
"Treat others the way they want to be treated."

That shift in awareness changes the way you communicate, how you lead and how you build trust that lasts.

Individually, these tools are useful.

Together, they build trust so people lean in and choose to follow.
You don't need to walk around with a checklist of soft skills.

You just need to stay anchored in what really matters — clear communication, mutual respect and genuine connection.

Because it's not about being perfect. It's about being present.
It's about being aware.

When you lead with intention — even in the small moments — you change how people feel.

And when people feel respected and included, they're far more likely to rise — bringing their best to the work and to each other.

That's the quiet power of emotional intelligence.
And that's what makes soft skills essential.

The real work? It's in how you show up.
Every moment is a chance to practice.

To be the reason someone feels heard.

The people who get this right don't just communicate better.

They lead better. Build better. Work better together.

That's where real impact begins.

The Quiet Power

It was my first corporate job — a small slice of a national account in a high-visibility region.

And one standout leader: Mike S.

He didn't posture. He didn't micromanage.
He was calm, clear and consistent — the same person whether things were on track or under pressure.

Mike set expectations from the start.
Roles were clear. KPIs were front and center.

He checked in, but he also left the proverbial door open for questions, concerns and clarifications.

He trusted us to own our projects and make decisions — and because that confidence was paired with clarity, we could deliver.

That support gave me the courage to make a tough call: replacing a vendor who was mishandling materials and slowing progress.

We were on a tight deadline, but Mike listened to my reasoning, backed the decision and moved forward without blame or second-guessing.

Soon after, a long-lead, custom-made product began arriving short at multiple locations.
Deadlines and budgets were suddenly at risk.

The first reaction could've been finger-pointing. Instead, Mike kept us focused on the outcome.

Together, we traced the problem to its source: the vendor had been working from a reduced copy of the original plans — which skewed measurements and takeoffs — an error that, left unchecked, would have multiplied across every site.

Because Mike led with presence, empathy and clarity, we caught the issue early, kept the project on track and stayed within budget—keeping both momentum and morale strong.

It was proof that when people skills are strong, performance takes care of itself.

That was just one project. One team.

Now imagine that same clarity, confidence and respect multiplied across every team, every project, every leader.

Performance strengthens.
Collaboration deepens.
People grow.

Soft skills are the catalyst.

They turn intention into action and action into results that last.

People and companies feel the difference.

That's the quiet power at work.

**With Heartfelt Thanks,**

To my husband, Rich and my children — Jamessina, Matthew and Keith — thank you for always being in my corner!

And Matthew, thank you for reviewing so many drafts. Your honest and thoughtful feedback made for enlightening conversations and great edits!

And to Frankie Redmond III for your thoughtful, detailed feedback. Your insights helped me keep chapters I was on the verge of cutting—and the book is better for it.

And to Kevin Engholm, for reviewing this book and offering thoughtful suggestions that brought clarity to the finish. I'm grateful our paths crossed when they did.

Available in paperback, ebook, and bulk digital formats.

Volume discounts for teams, training programs and corporate rollouts.

SoftSkills-101.com/bulk